The Painless Path to
PROPER PUNCTUAT

PROF. PERRY'S
POPULAR PEDAGOGICAL PICTORIALS
Proudly Presents

The Painless Path to
PROPER PUNCTUATION

OR

Who Killed Albert the Crook?

AN OFFICIAL PROF. PERRY U-SOLVE-IT CRIME CLASSIC

Ably Arranged, Edited, and Illustrated by

Stan Malotte

St. Martin's Press   New York

USER'S NOTE
In addition to the main text, an appendix in the back explains finer points for each
punctuation mark, and a complete index quickly locates discussion
of each mark's various uses.

THE PAINLESS PATH TO PROPER PUNCTUATION. Copyright © 1990 by Stan Malotte. All rights
reserved. Printed in the United States of America. No part of this book may be used or
reproduced in any manner whatsoever without written permission except in the case
of brief quotations embodied in critical articles or reviews. For information, address
St. Martin's Press, 175 Fifth Avenue, New York, N.Y. 10010.

Library of Congress Cataloging-in-Publication Data
Malotte, Stan.
 The painless path to proper punctuation, or, Who killed Albert the
Crook? / Stan Malotte.
  p.   cm.
 "A Thomas Dunne book."
 ISBN 0-312-04399-6
 1. English language—Punctuation—Humor.   I. Title.
PE1450.M335   1990
428.2—dc20   89-77077
                                                              CIP

First Edition
10 9 8 7 6 5 4 3 2 1

For Lisa

Contents

Preface

For his book, Prof. Perry has adopted the punctuation standards commonly taught in our high school and college texts. These standards are important, he says, because correct punctuation yields clear writing, and clear writing is only common courtesy. "Two thousand years ago," says Prof. Perry, "there was no such thing as punctuation and everybody died. Good nutrition is also important, but I am convinced that witho . . ."

Thank you, Professor.

Prof. Perry has asked that each owner of his book be congratulated on taking this major step toward achieving clear—and courteous—writing; writing, writing.

—S.M.

U-SOLVE-IT
Directions

Prof. Perry has chosen to present his guidance in the context of a crime that escaped the notice of newspapers throughout the world: the fatal murder of Albert the Crook. As the investigation proceeds, all clues necessary to the crime's solution are given. The reader will know everything Bill the Detective knows and should be able to name the murderer just before Bill announces his identity. The opportunity to do so is given on page 123.

Prior peeking past that page is not permitted.

The Painless Path to *PROPER PUNCTUATION*

Chapter I
THE PERIOD

PERIOD
AT REST
1942

Period

A period is used (1) to end a complete sentence—"complete" meaning with at least a subject and verb, as in: *Someone* [subject] *murdered* *Albert the Crook* [object]. (2) to end a phrase like "Oh dear." (3) and even a single word like "Hm."

3

Period

The period also is used in abbreviations that could be mistaken for ordinary words—e.g., write *cap*. (for "capital"), not *cap* (a hat); *prod*. (for "producer"), not *prod* (to push); *fig*. (for "figure"), *C.O.D.*, and so forth. A general rule is that abbreviations formed by omitting letters usually have a period—e.g., *secty.*, *Mrs.*, *agcy.*, and many others.* Contractions like *3rd*, *18th*, *it's*, *can't*, and so on, do not have periods.

*British usage omits these periods.

5

Period

Periods in Latin-derived abbreviations help remind us of their origin. Other useful examples are *N.B.* or *n.b.* (*nota bene*: "note well"), *et al.* (*et alii*: "and others"), and others.

7

Period

The period in an abbreviation also can act as the period for the end of the sentence, as the period in "etc." does at right. Also note that the exclamation point after "London!" serves as the ending punctuation for that sentence. Double punctuation is not needed.*

*Double punctuation *would* occur in, say, a list of books if one of them already has an ending mark in its title, as in: *Moby-Dick*, *Help!*, *The Crisis*.

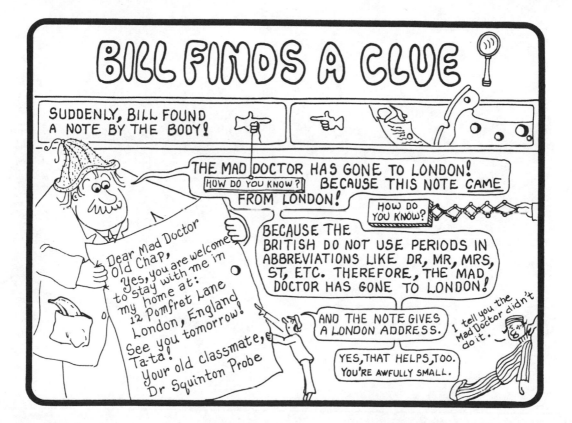

9

Chapter II
THE COMMA

HALLEY'S
COMMA
1986

Comma

A comma follows the greeting in a letter, as in *Dear Louise,* or *Hi Bert,* etc. However, the greeting in a business or formal letter is followed by a colon, as in *Dear Madame:* or *Dear Dr. Sigmoid:* or *To whom it may concern:* and so forth.

13

Comma

A comma goes after the letter's goodbye (the complimentary close) in both friendly and business letters. (Also note the comma before the added-on "isn't it?" in Bill's balloon at far right.)

BILL HELPS OUT
PARDON ME, SIR. IT'S NONE OF MY BUSINESS, BUT IT SHOULD BE "DEAR PILOT COMMA."
HREE-ALLY?
AND AT THE END, BE SURE TO PUT A COMMA AFTER THE GOODBYE LINE—LIKE "YOURS TRULY COMMA" IN A BUSINESS LETTER, OR MAYBE "SO LONG FOR NOW COMMA" IN A FRIENDLY LETTER.
THIS IS A FRIENDLY LETTER, ISN'T IT?
HI YAM FR-R-IENDLY—EEF THEY LET ME!
BILL FELT
STRANGELY UNEASY

Comma

We usually think of "ham and eggs" as a single breakfast item, but the comma in the example at right changes that. Also *see* pages 18, 20, 24.

17

Comma

For clarity, a comma should go before the final *and* in a series. Also *see* pages 16, 20, 24.

Comma

The final comma in a series avoids even the briefest moment of confusion—which is only common courtesy to the reader. At the right, for example, one of the choices in number 3 is clearly not "liver and onions and ham." (Prof. Perry recommends the final comma in a series even in such a short sentence as *The flag is red, white, and blue.*)

DISASTER AVERTED

SUDDENLY, A HUSH CAME OVER THE PASSENGERS AS BILL STRODE TO THE FRONT OF THE CABIN.

THIS IS REALLY QUITE SIMPLE TO RESOLVE.

1. muffins al fresco, liver and onions, ham, and eggs
(CLEAR: means <u>four</u> separate dishes)

2. muffins al fresco, liver and onions, ham and eggs
(FAIRLY CLEAR: <u>three</u> separate dishes, but could mean more)

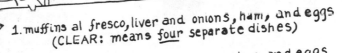

3. muffins al fresco, liver and onions, and ham and eggs
(BEST: clearly means <u>three</u> separate dishes)

HM.

HM.

HM.

HM.

Comma

A comma is used following an introductory element as at right in "Ladees and people, don't . . ." (direct address), and in such other cases as *All right, I won't leave the plane!* and *Well, he's only pretending!* and *Maybe, but look at his hair!*

Comma

At right, a comma is needed after "plugs." The final comma is especially helpful in long, complex series containing several *and*'s or other conjunctions. Commas are not used in a series when each item is connected by a coordinating conjunction: *The house was full of horses and chickens and cows*.

Comma

Like an introductory word or phrase, an introductory clause needs a comma after it so the reader instantly knows the next word is not part of the introductory part. The terrorist's note should read: "Because it is so crowded inside, the passengers . . ." (The inverted order of the clauses in that sentence is another hint that a comma is needed.)

A CRUCIAL OMISSION

Comma

Interrupters like *furthermore** should be set off by commas. The note should read: "I demand, furthermore, that . . ." Another interrupter in the sentence is "except for commercials" which also should be set off by commas. (Another problem with this sentence is discussed on the next page.)

---

*Also: *etc., therefore, of course, perhaps, as a matter of fact, too, nevertheless, however,* and others. BUT: *However you came, you shall return in my private yacht.*

Comma

The words "full" and "uninterrupted" each separately describes (modifies) the single concept "prime time hour" (think of it as a single word: primetimehour), so a comma goes after "full" but not after "uninterrupted." A general rule is that if *and* can be placed between the adjectives in a series without sounding awkward, use a comma; if not, don't.

Comma

A comma goes before *and after* the year in a complete date, and before *and after* the state in a place name. The entry should read: "We were flying April 3, 1990, over Rahway, New Jersey, when we were . . . ," etc.* The same rule applies to abbreviations after names, as in: *Squinton Probe, M.D., lives in London, but Squinton Probe, Jr., does not.* (BUT: In *Squinton Probe, Jr.'s horse*, the "Jr.'s" needs no comma after it.) Commas are not used with numerals: *King Henry VIII is not related in any way to Willard Kookyboodle VIII.*

---

*A partial date (e.g., *April 1990*) doesn't use commas; nor does the day-month-year style (e.g., *3 April 1990*). A ZIP code in an address has no comma before it.

33

Comma

A word, phrase, or clause that follows a word and gives more information about it, called an *appositive*, is set off by commas. Therefore, the alien's speech at right should read: "... *Fido*, an intergalactic ..." and "... the good ship *Rover*, an intergalactic ..." Some appositives are not set off by commas. Consider: *My sister Ann arrived early*. No commas around "Ann" means the speaker has several sisters and is specifying which one. Compare: *My sister, Ann, arrived early*. The commas indicate that the speaker has only one sister and that the name is merely added as helpful but not essential information.

35

Comma

A comma appears after "away" in the alien's speech at right in order to signal the reader that the first idea is complete and that a brand new sentence is starting after the "and." The rule is: a comma goes between two independent clauses joined by a coordinating conjunction (*and*, *but*, *for*, *or*, *nor*, *so*, or *yet*). The result is a *compound sentence*. A very short compound sentence, like *Bill stood and the others sat*, doesn't need the comma because the eye can scan the whole sentence without danger of incorrectly anticipating future words. Punctuation helps keep the reader on-track.

THE ALIENS' SECRET PLAN!
We mean you no harm. Our craft has come from a planet trillions of miles away, and we have come to your planet to seek people samples.
Are you "people"?
NG23
SHE IS!
HE IS!
SHE IS!
HE IS!
HE IS!
SHE IS!
THEY ARE!
HE IS!
HE IS!
HE IS!
HE IS!
THEY ARE!
WOOF!

Comma

If the two verbs, even in a long compound sentence, share the same subject, as in Bill's speech at right (which has "I" for its subject), the comma is not used before the "and."

THE PASSENGERS SUBMIT

"SIR, I WOULD LIKE TO SPEAK FOR THE GROUP AND ASK WHAT YOU PLAN TO DO WITH YOUR "PEOPLE SAMPLES."

HE'S "PEOPLE"!

HE'S "PEOPLE"!

THEY'RE "PEOPLE"!

SHE'S "PEOPLE"!

HE'S "PEOP[LE]"!

we will give them great quantities of earth money as a test of their character.

AND SO AM I!

39

Comma

The comma after "ask" in the terrorist's first speech at right is needed because the clause introduces a question. A similar case would be: *He wondered, What are the possibilities here?* A capital letter to start the question part is optional, but helps the reader if it is a long question. Quotation marks aren't needed around the question part because it is not conversation. However, the marks would be used if he were quoting himself from something he'd said in the past (e.g., *All I can remember is asking her, "Will you marry me?"*)

Comma

American English, unlike British English, uses the comma in four-digit numbers like 2,143 or 9,800 or 1,200, etc. The comma signals the reader that the figure is a number instead of a year, as in: *In 1989, 1,989 people were born in our town.* (The sentence would be even better if recast to separate the numbers: *In 1989, there were 1,989 births in our town.*) Page numbers do not use a comma: *It appears on page 1289 and again on page 11943.*

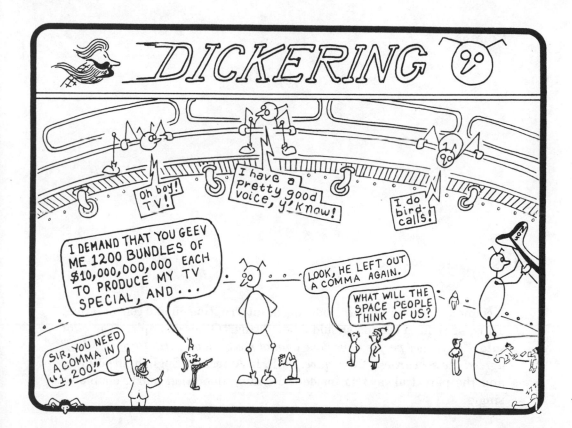

Comma

A comma is needed when introducing or interrupting quoted conversation. Thus, at right, a comma should follow "sang." Other examples: *The pilot said, "The space people have done a lot of research on earth things." "Yes," agreed the stewardess, "they have."* N.B. In American English, the comma and the period always go inside the ending quotation mark, double or single.

THE ALIENS SUBMIT

...AND I FURTHER DEMAND THAT YOU FLY THEES SPACESHIP TO LONDON!

London! Oh good! I've always wanted to see Disneyland!

And meet Shakespeare!

Ah yes! It was his immortal Hamlet who sang "I am the captain of the Pinafore, and a right good cap..."

PARDON ME, SIR, A COMMA GOES AFTER "SANG."

That's not Shakespeare.

I didn't say it.

oh boy!

45

Comma

Without commas, the clause "who sing best" at right is a *restrictive* clause; that is, it restricts, or defines, the *kind* of tall people who will be hired (the ones who sing best), but it says nothing about *not* hiring other kinds of people, short or tall. If commas were added—"The tall people, who sing best, will be hired."—only tall people would be hired, because the commas make the clause "who sing best" *non-restrictive*, i.e., merely an added opinion that could be left out because it would not be essential to the main point of the sentence.

47

Comma

A comma is needed when an omitted word is to be understood. The alien's speech at right should read: "No no! Gilbert and Sullivan wrote *The Pinafore*; Shakespeare, *Hamlet*." The comma after "Shakespeare" reminds the reader of the omitted word "wrote." Another example: *The passengers are tiny; the space people, quite large.** Usually, commas are not needed in short expressions like *The more the merrier* or *The sooner the better*. BUT: *Cold hands, warm heart*.

*Note the semicolon after "tiny" to avoid a *comma splice*. (See Appendix, page 139.)

GETTING IT STRAIGHT
Where is everybo
Now try to remember: Shakespeare wrote Hamlet.
Oh, that's right. Then who wrote The Pinafore?
No no! Gilbert and Sulliva Shakespeare rote The Pinafore; Shakespeare Hamle
SIR, YOU NEED A COMMA BETWEEN "SHAKESPEARE" AND "HAMLET."
They'll know in London!
Hey! It's empty back here!

Comma

The possible confusion when identical words occur together is avoided by the comma between them. The alien should say: "Yes sir, I was going to, to take us to London." Another example: *Whoever will, will succeed*. A comma, however, should not be used in: *I hope that that won't be confusing* or *If he had had this book, the problem would not have occurred*.

51

Chapter III
THE VIRGULE

VIRGULE
VIEWING
GRAND CANYON
(not shown)

Virgule

The virgule (also called a *slash*, *solidus*, or *slant mark*) is used to show alternatives by meaning *or* in such combinations as *his/her*, *and/or*, *air-plane/UFO*, et al. Its second common use is as a substitute for the word *per* as in *4 min./qt.* or *93,000 mi./hr.*

*A highly volatile form of condensed gravity used as fuel.

Virgule

When poetry is written in run-on sentence form instead of in separate lines, the poem's line-breaks are shown by virgules with a space on each side, as in the lady's poem at right which should appear as follows: The next time we roam / Will be around home / From kitchen to basement, and then, / If we start to get weary, / I'll just say, "Now, dearie, / Let's plan a trip to the den!"

57

*ZGRF IS FOUND IN ABUNDANCE AT THE NORTH POLE.
†AN IMPORTANT LIFE CONCEPT.

Chapter IV
THE
EXCLAMATION POINT

EXCLAMATION
POINT AT
BLASTOFF

Exclamation Point

At right, Bill is right. Those aboard the spaceship failed to reflect the excitement of the moment by using exclamation points after their statements. Words expressing strong feeling, whether one word or a whole sentence, should be followed by an exclamation point. All speech balloons except Bill's should have their marks. The picture's title should, too! The spaceship itself is the only participant that used the mark appropriately. N.B. For placement of the "!" with other punctuation, *see* pages 68–69.

61

Chapter V
THE
QUESTION MARK

EXCLAMATION
POINT AFTER
BLASTOFF

Question Mark

The question mark follows direct questions, quoted or imaginary (e.g., *"Where are we?" he asked. Where are we? he wondered. The question was, Where were they?*).* Indirect questions do not take a mark (e.g., *He's wondering where we are*). Bill's poster shows how to handle a question within question: Only one mark is needed. Also note that Bill's polite request that everyone gather around him needs no question mark.

*An unquoted single-word question at the end of a sentence needs no question mark, as in *He wondered why*. (BUT: *Why? he wondered*.)

Question Mark

When used to indicate uncertainty in dates, the question mark follows the questioned date without an intervening space. When used in parentheses to question a word in a sentence, again there is no space. The question mark in brackets, [?], is sometimes used to express irony, as in *The young lady's singing* [?] *could be heard throughout the airplane*. However, beware of this device which can seem like mere sarcasm.

A HOPEFUL SIGN
A SIGN! I FOUND A SIGN!
WHAT THE SIGN SAID
NOTICE HOW THE QUESTION MARK SHOWS UNCERTAINTY ABOUT THE YEAR OF MR. KOOKYBOODLE'S BIRTH.
IN TRIBUTE TO ASA KOOKYBOODLE [1636?–1697]
First man to find the North Pole and then misplace it. It should be around here(?) somewhere.
IT'S BLANK
And whoever made the sign wasn't sure if the North Pole is really around "here"!
Hm.
Hm.
HEY! LOOK HERE! WE'RE SAVED! SAVED!

Question Mark

The comma and period go *inside* ending quotation marks. The colon and semicolon go *outside*. The question mark and exclamation point, however, can go inside or outside depending on whether they relate to the whole sentence or to just a part of it.

Compare: *Who said, "Don't give up the ship"?*

He said, "May I give up the ship?"

AN INFLATED HOPE

69

Chapter VI
THE ELLIPSIS

"THE MARK THAT COULD REPLACE
THE LIBRARY OF CONGRESS"
from Yes! We Can Cut
Government Spending!

Ellipsis

Broken, confused speech is indicated by the ellipsis (plural: ellipses). (Broken speech that contains strong sudden changes of thought uses the dash [*see* pages 118–19].) The ellipsis is principally used to show where words have been omitted when condensing quoted matter. For instance, in the picture at right someone apparently replaced the original worn-out flag with a new one that was too small to contain all of the original message.

Chapter VII
THE HYPHEN

SUSPENDED
HYPHEN
from Powers of the
Ancient Druids

Hyphen

At right, ". . . ten- or twenty-mile-deep . . ." needs a hyphen and a space after "ten" (called a *suspended hyphen*) because "ten" is intended to become a *compound modifier* with the words "mile-deep" just like "twenty-mile-deep." The hyphen alerts the reader to that fact, and saves repeating "mile-deep." A temporary* *compound word* like "English-speakers" needs a hyphen; otherwise, it would mean speakers who are English, not necessarily speakers of English.

See Appendix, page 142.

Hyphen

Spelled-out numbers from twenty-one through ninety-nine need hyphens, as do fractions—e.g., *two-thirds*, *one-half*—irrespective of how they are used in a sentence. Words that are visually confusing (like "belllike") or that could have their meanings confused (like *re-cover* vs. *recover*, *re-sign* vs. *resign*) also need hyphens.

Hyphen

The hyphen is used with numbers, times, and dates to mean "from-to."* So, at right, either delete the "from" or write "from 5 to 60 minutes." The same applies to dates. Nobody *lived from 1807–1882*. Use plain *lived 1807–1882* or *lived from 1807 to 1882*. Also with times: *The meeting is scheduled for 9:30–11* or *from 9:30 to 11*—not *from 9:30–11*.

*In typesetting, an *en dash* is used for this purpose. *See* Appendix, page 143.

Chapter VIII
THE COLON

●

●

TYPICAL COLON
OF THE 1940's
from Colon Design
through the Ages

Colon

The colon provides a sentence with a set-up/payoff structure. For example, at right, "following" needs a colon after it because it introduces a list. A colon is needed after "lies ahead" because the first part of that sentence sets up a promise, and the rest of the sentence pays off. **(Avoid the common error of using a semicolon for a colon.)**

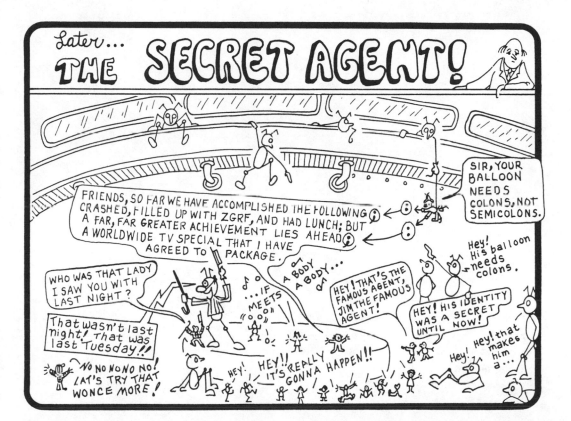

85

Chapter IX

THE

APOSTROPHE

HALLEY'S
APOSTROPHE
DUE 2061

Apostrophe

Although singular words normally form possessives with *'s*, certain names ending in <u>s</u> traditionally don't—e.g., write *Jesus' teachings*, *Moses' laws*, *Xerxes'*, *Rameses'*, et al., because of the extra <u>s</u> sound in such words. The construction "for righteousness's sake" tends to seize the tongue, so leave off the final <u>s</u> there, too. However, if combinations like "Francis's Shoe Store" seem simple to say, Prof. Perry would permit it.

Apostrophe

Men is already plural, as are *ladies* and *children*. Therefore, there are no such things as *Mens Clothing*, *Ladies Hats*, and *Childrens Shoes*. There are only *Men's Clothing, Ladies' Hats, and Children's Shoes.* Anyone wearing any of the former can be recognized by a slight list to their walk. In the example showing joint possession, the possessive is used only with "Ladies": "Men and Ladies' Bus Seat Race." If there were separate races, it would read: "Men's and Ladies' Bus Seat Races."

91

Apostrophe

One of the most common errors is using the contraction *it's* ("it is") in place of the possessive pronoun *its*. Also, there are no such forms as *its'* or *ours'* or *your's* or *hers'* or *their's*, et al. Just remember the difference between *contractions* where the apostrophe replaces a missing letter— as in *it's* ("it is"), *who's* ("who is"), *he's* ("he is"), *isn't* ("is not"), *you're* ("you are"), and so on—and *possessive pronouns* that are words of their own (like *its*, *whose*, *yours*, *ours*, *theirs*, *his*, and *hers*).

93

Chapter X
THE
ASTERISK

EXCLAMATION
POINT AT
IMPACT

Asterisk

For occasional footnotes, use the *asterisk system* instead of the small *superior numbers system* ([1], [2], [3], etc.) that is used for extensively footnoted materials. If there is more than one footnote on a page, the asterisk system employs the following symbols in this order: * (asterisk), † (dagger), ‡ (double dagger), § (section mark), ‖ (parallels), # (number sign). If more are needed, simply double them in the same sequence.

*This is the footnote indicated by the asterisk after "CRASH." Because it is not in the frame of the actual drawing above, it is unlikely the search crew will find it.

Chapter XI
PARENTHESES
&
BRACKETS

( ) [ ]

DEUX FEMMES
— Picasso

DEUX FEMMES
— Mondrian

Parentheses & Brackets

At right, parentheses are needed around "see page 9" because it is really just an aside—incidental information that could be left out without disturbing the sentence's meaning. "Big Long Awful Missile" appears in parentheses as a helpful explanation or reminder of the meaning of "BLAM."

101

Parentheses & Brackets

Brackets are used to indicate words added by the editor that are not in the original. Such additions can correct, explain, or comment, as in Miss Edna's plaque at right.

Parentheses & Brackets

If another parenthetical statement appears inside the first one, use brackets. The space creature's statement at right should read: ". . . our UFO fleet (all Class 3 StarTwinkles [*UFO Trends* calls them 'The FunSaucer'] with the new thicker paint to hold them together) will soon be . . ." If still another parenthetical statement goes inside the bracketed one, use parentheses again, and so on.

Chapter XII
THE SEMICOLON

A WHOLE
SEMICOLON

Semicolon

Normally, in a compound sentence, a comma separates two independent clauses joined by such coordinating conjunctions as *but*, *and*, *or*, *nor*, and *for* (e.g.: *Bill realized the Mad Doctor was incapable of murder, but then who could have killed Albert the Crook?*). However, when there are already commas in those separate clauses, use a semicolon to separate. Thus, at right, there should be a semicolon after "Nuthatch."

Semicolon

A common use of the semicolon is to join closely related independent clauses that have no conjunction, as in the clue note at right. Such clauses could be written as two separate sentences (as in Bill's comment), but the semicolon keeps them related. A period, for example, between the two clauses in the clue note would weaken the close relationship. Very short related clauses or phrases, however, can be joined by a comma for easier flow (*Easy come, easy go*) or by no mark at all (*The more the merrier*).

Semicolon

Semicolons are used to keep a close relationship between independent clauses that use transitional words like *however*, *nevertheless*, *therefore*, *besides*, *namely*, and so on. Also, a semicolon is used before transitional abbreviations like *e.g.* ("for example") and *i.e.** ("that is"), as in the "CLUE #2" note. Also note that a comma follows the transitional word or abbreviation.

*Avoid the common error of using *i.e.* for *e.g. E.g.* is used to set up a specific example (*He owned odd things, e.g., a whole-wheat rainbow*); *i.e.* is used to introduce an explanation in different words (*Some thought him unsettled, i.e., loony*).

A BUSY DAY
MASH!
READY TO SHOOT THE TERRORIST'S STATEMENT! WHERE'S MAKEUP!
YESSIR, TAKING OVER THE WORLD TAKES MONEY, HOWEVER, YOUR TAX-DEDUCTIBLE CONTRIBUTION CAN HELP US HELP YOU BY HELPING OURSELVES...
...EVERY LASSIE HAS HER LADDIE; NINE, THEY SAY, HA' I...
CUT! CUT! CUT!
A SEMICOLON! RIGHT, CHIEF?
SUDDENLY: CLUE #2!
(WHAT THE NOTE SAID)
• CLUE #2 •
Dear Bill, You know me; i.e., you think you know me.

Semicolon

If there are commas within items in a list, the items should be separated by semicolons. Thus, the terrorist's balloon at right should read: ". . . me, Emperor; Lassie, Chief Dog; Heidi, Secretary of Sunshine; [etc.]." (In such series, also use a semicolon before the final item.) The need for semicolons is even more obvious in a sentence like: *He arranged them in groups of three: pigs, cows, chickens; horses, ducks, geese; and penguins, axolotls, and ukeleles.*

The Terrorist's Demands
THIS IS RIDICULOUS!
YES! WHERE ARE HIS SEMICOLONS?
...AND EVERYBODY IN THEE WORLD MUST AGREE, UNDER PENALTY OF WORKING IN A PRESTIGE POSITION, TO LEARN TO TAP-DANCE. FURTHERMORE, I WEEL APPOINT THE FOLLOWING PEEPUL TO RULE THEE WORLD: ME, EMPEROR, LASSIE, CHIEF DOG, HEIDI, SECRETARY OF SUNSHINE ...
I THOUGHT WE WERE GOING TO RULE THE WORLD.

Chapter XIII
THE DASH

THE DASH
from *Punctuation Exercises*

Dash

Dashes are correctly used in the "CLUE #3" note to set off a sudden, strong change in thought.* Another example would be: *A slight pressure—perhaps there had been an explosion several miles away—was sensed by the alert Bill*. The dash also is correctly used in the "CLUE #36" note to introduce a summary statement. N.B. To indicate a dash on the typewriter, use two hyphens.

*See pages 72–73 for use of ellipses in broken, confused thought.

119

Dash

The three things that Bill realized at far right are correctly set off by dashes because they comprise a long *appositive*—words that further identify or explain the word just before them—and especially because this appositive contains other punctuation (i.e., commas). *See* Appendix under *Dash*, pages 150–151, for discussion of when to choose dashes instead of commas or parentheses.

Helpful Hints

Yes, Bill knows who the murderer is! With a whisk of his pen, he will change the punctuation in the note at right only slightly and reveal the malefactor! The clues are all there:

- The murderer must be among those who can't read French or he would have known the real title of Sartre's book is *Life Is **Not** a Golf Game*. However, no one in this whole book can read French.

- The omission of a comma after the greeting points directly to the terrorist! However—

- The incorrect use of the semicolon where a colon should be points to Jim the Agent, who had trouble with that mark on page 109! But—

- The omission of quotation marks around "final green" (who can miss that reference to money! Ha!) points to someone who knows the hiding place of the loot stolen by Albert the Crook! And that could be anyone! And—

- If "final green" has a double meaning, perhaps something else in the sentence does, too—and also needs quotation marks! And Bill knows what that is and therefore the name of the murderer of Albert the Crook!

Do You?

Attention, Reader!
DO NOT TURN THIS PAGE

With the final clue below, you the reader now know everything Bill knows (possibly more) and should be able to solve the crime! Read the following clue carefully. Do not turn this page until you have decided who the murderer is.
(If you like, you may read HELPFUL HINTS! on the page at left.)
BUT FIRST, READ THE CLUE NOTE BELOW

CLUE #95

Dear Bill
Try this clue from *Life Is a Golf Game*
by Jean-Paul Sartre;

HOLES IN ONE ARE NOTHING BUT WAYS
TO GET TO THE FINAL GREEN FASTER.

Guess who!

Ready? Write your decision on a piece of paper and then destroy it.
NOW TURN THE PAGE!

Chapter XIV

QUOTATION MARKS
(DOUBLE and SINGLE)

HALLEY'S
APOCALYPSE

Quotation Marks

Direct quotations in dialogue are set off by double quotation marks. A quotation within the quotation is set off by single marks. (The British reverse this system.) Quotation marks are not used for indirect quotes as in Bill's "I started to say no, but then . . ." Also note the position of other punctuation. The comma goes inside the ending quotation mark—even before the single mark in a case like: *"Then you say, 'I do,' " she explained.* A question mark is placed to relate to the actual question being asked, as in Bill's final question at right—which, of course, needs only the one question mark. (Also *see* page 65.)

Quotation Marks

Quotation marks are used to indicate special treatment of words to show they have an unexpected meaning, as in "holes in one" at right. They also are used to define a foreign word (e.g., *The word* zgrf *means "mayonnaise"*),* to set off an unfamiliar word (e.g., *An "en" is a printer's measure*), to indicate nicknames like Andrew "Old Hickory" Jackson (but not everyday nicknames like Butch or Dopey, or a descriptive term as in Stonewall Jackson), and to express irony (e.g., *That prisoner there was one of our more "promising" politicians*).

*Also *see* page 150.

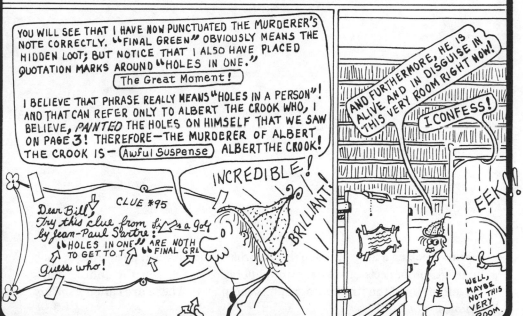

Quotation Marks

When quoting a long passage that is broken into several paragraphs, each paragraph or section starts with a quotation mark, but the ending mark is left off until the final paragraph is completed. These are called *running quotes*.

From an actual copy —

THE MURDERER'S CONFESSION

THE TERRORIST ALIAS ALBERT THE CROOK!

"BILL IS RIGHT! I PAINTED THE HOLES TO PRETEND I WAS DEAD SO NO ONE WOULD FOLLOW ME TO THE HIDDEN LOOT!

I THOUGHT SHE WAS ONLY A LOGO

"BUT I AM NOT REALLY THE TERRORIST OR ALBERT THE CROOK. I AM REALLY MISS EDNA!

"BUT THAT WAS A DISGUISE, TOO! IN REALITY, I AM HUGH THE HOPEFUL ACTOR. THE TERRORIST BUSINESS WAS JUST A WAY TO GET NATIONAL TV EXPOSURE.

"AND BEING AN ACTOR—WELL, THAT WAS JUST A WAY TO DISGUISE MY DEEPEST SELF-DOUBTS.

"AND MY SELF-DOUBT WAS JUST A WAY TO CONCEAL MY INCREDIBLE EGO.

"AND NOW, I DON'T KNOW WHO I AM. I MUST FIND MYSELF. OH, PLEASE HELP ME."

Appendix

PERIOD

Page 2   Periods, not question marks, are used to end sentences that may seem like questions but are not:

Bill asked if anyone liked his hat. [indirect question]

Isn't it a lovely day. [rhetorical question]

Would you please get off my foot. [polite request]

Page 4   Most abbreviations like *Tues.*, *30 mph*, and so on, are not used in formal writing. Exceptions are common titles like *Mr.*, *Dr.*, *Jr.*, *Ph.D.*, et al.

Page 6   There is no period after the *et* in *et al.* because *et* is the complete Latin word for "and," not an abbreviation. Compare *ad lib.*, *id est*, and others.

- *Vertical lists and outlines:* Periods follow the letters or numbers that begin items, but periods or other punctuation do not follow the items themselves unless one or more of the items is a complete sentence. Compare:

Bill knew the following:
    a. The victim's condition
    b. The time (give or take a few days)

Bill's observations:
    a. The victim was not happy.
    b. It was a pleasant day.

- When typing abbreviations, do not space between letters (*e.g., i.e., Ph.D., N.Car.*); however, in people's names, use a space between the initials (*G. B. Shaw, C. S. Lewis*).

- Periods are not needed after postal abbreviations (*NY, CA*), chapter titles and other display lines (as in advertising), or after newspaper story headlines.

- The period is omitted after sentences quoted within another sentence:

  The sentences "I am a spy," "I am not a spy," and "I am a liar" seem confusing when written in sequence.

COMMA

Page 12 Because of the colon-quote mark combination (:") that follows "concern" in the last sentence, the addition of a comma (normally needed before the tagged-on phrase "and so forth") would be a third mark of punctuation and therefore more confusing than requiring the reader to mentally supply it. Always take the route of least confusion.

Scholarly writing, however, can require triple or even quadruple punctuation; but when you're that advanced, it's time to buy a good style book like *The Chicago Manual of Style*.

Page 22 Without the comma after introductory elements, problems like this occur:

In the winter time is not so easily judged by the sun if it's snowing.

A comma is needed after "winter."

Tag-ons (as well as introductory elements) need commas:

MILLICENT: You're Fred, aren't you?
FRED: I am Millicent!

A comma is needed before "Millicent." [direct address]

A comma is not needed when the verb comes right after the introductory phrase. Compare:

Through the wall came the sound of voices.

Through the wall, he could hear voices.

General rule: Inverted order is often the reason a comma is needed. For example, the second sentence above is really an inversion of *He could hear voices through the wall*. We also use a comma when names are inverted: *Smith, John.*

Page 28 *Contrasting expressions* are another type of interrupter that should be set off by commas:

> *Bill decided the terrorist, not the stewardess, was the one with the mustache.*

Page 30 Separating descriptive adjectives by commas in the right places is important. Compare:

> *a large, old stone house*
> [means a stone house that is large and old]

> *a large old stone house*
> [might be misinterpreted as a large house made of old stones (in which case, however, "old-stone" should be hyphenated)]

Page 36 A comma is not used before *but* when it means "except." Compare:

> *Everyone came but Sam and Sue.* [means "except"]

> *Everyone came, but Sam and Sue stayed home.* [means "however"]

Page 41 There is no comma after the interjection "Oh" in the alien's "Oh yes" because such phrases have become a single unit by usage. Others are *Ah my dear*, *Oh yeah!* and *Now then*.

Page 46 Proverbial elements often contain restrictive elements, as in *He who is wise is rich*. The clause "who is wise" is essential to the sentence's meaning and therefore not set off by commas.

Miscellaneous

- Beware the *comma splice*:

  WRONG: *He ran home, he expected a call any minute.*

  RIGHT: *He ran home; he expected a call any minute.*

Without the conjunction *because* after "home," a semicolon is needed to signal the reader that the first complete thought of the compound sentence is finished and a new thought is coming. A comma misleads the reader to expect more of the first thought. Although making two separate sentences would be correct (if a choppy style is being used on purpose), the semicolon keeps the two thoughts related.

- If comma use (or any punctuation use) gets out of hand, recast the sentence. For instance, the sentence

  Because I asked the question, "Did anyone hear a bomb ticking?" early lunch was called.

might be better recast as an indirect question:

  Because I asked if anyone heard a bomb ticking, early lunch was called.

VIRGULE

Miscellaneous

- The virgule is also used to show overlapping time periods:

    He was briefly a senator (1912/1913), and then ...

EXCLAMATION POINT

Miscellaneous

- In avoiding double punctuation, the exclamation point often overwhelms the question mark:

    Who yelled "Fire!"

- Don't overuse the exclamation point; your writing might seem like meaningless advertising (*At last! Sensational! Mediocre!*), or, if used in brackets for editorial comment, merely snide (*We have created [!] a new bus schedule*).

QUESTION MARK

Miscellaneous

- A question in parentheses showing the thought process of a character needs a question mark, but no quotation marks:

    He heard a sound (was it the wind?) and turned.

- A series of alternatives each takes a question mark:

    What should we do if it rains? snows? clears up?

ELLIPSIS

Miscellaneous

- If the end of a sentence occurs during an omission indicated by an ellipsis, add a fourth dot as the period—or a question mark or exclamation point as appropriate.

    However, an ellipsis after a purposely incomplete sentence (in dialogue, for instance) does not take a period. Two examples occur on page 79.

- In quoted conversation showing confused speech, the ellipsis is followed by a comma as in normal quoted speech:

    "I ... I mean ...," Wendell began.

- An ellipsis is seldom necessary to show omitted matter at the beginning of a quotation since it is taken for granted that something came before.

- A full line of dots (*long ellipsis*) is used to indicate omission of a full line of poetry. The line of dots should be the same length as the line of poetry above it:

> *Roses are red,*
> *Violets are blue,*
>
> . . . . . .
> *And so are you.*

- The long ellipsis also is used to indicate omission of a whole paragraph or more of prose writing.

HYPHEN

Page 76 Hyphens connect compound words—either *temporary* ones like *Little-used spaceship for sale* [seldom flown] to distinguish it from *Little used spaceship for sale* [a used spaceship that is small]; or *permanent* ones like *free-for-all*, *left-handed*, *stick-in-the-mud*. Some permanent compounds have become even more permanent by ending up as solid words like *bookstore*, *weekend*, *spaceship*. A compound like *stick-in-the-mud*, however, will probably never become solid; but check the dictionary for a compound's current status.

Page 80 In printing, a hyphen won't be used in "from–to" constructions like "lived 1847–1889." Instead, the typesetter will set an *en dash* (a dash half the length of the normal full *em dash* and longer than the hyphen). When typing, use the hyphen; but if the material will be typeset, be sure to mark it to be an en dash.

Other uses of the en dash:

Bible addresses and page citations (*Gen 1:26–28*; *pages 12–14*)

Job title with sub-category (*Vice-President–Marketing*)

In place of a hyphen in combinations with compound words (*New York–Lancaster bus* [to avoid confusion with a *new* bus route from York to Lancaster])

To make a temporary compound of an already compound term (*pre–New World mentality*)

To join compounds into a new compound (*Ex-drinkers–Ex-smokers Banquet*)

Breaking words into syllables

The hyphen is used to break a word into syllables when a word breaks at the end of a line. One-syllable words like *helped* are not broken.

Check the dictionary for the correct breaks, but the following rules of thumb will help:

Rule 1. The hyphen usually comes after a long vowel:

long vowel	*short vowel*
na-tion	nat-u-ral
Po-land	pol-i-tics
gi-ant	gig-gle
fe-male	fem-i-nine
fu-ture	fun-da-men-tal

Rule 2. The *-le* stays with the consonant it follows (*wrin-kle*, *gig-gling*). Beware of exceptions like *pick-le*.

Rule 3. Words usually are broken the way they sound (*co-or-di-na-tion*, *an-nu-al*, *at-tack*). Note how two consonants are split.

Rule 4. The root word usually stays a unit (*danc-ing*, not "dan-cing").

Rule 5. Beware of confusing homographs (words spelled alike) such as *pro-duce/prod-uce*; *for-mer/form-er*.

Hyphenating prefixes

Certain prefixes usually take a hyphen after them: *self-*, *ex-*, *all-*, *ill-* (*self-conscious*, *ex-accountant*, *all-college*, *ill-mannered*), and others. However, when another prefix is added, the rule is ignored (e.g., *self-conscious* becomes *unselfconscious*).

Other prefixes take no hyphen (*nonessential*, *unwanted*, *semiarid*, *midnight*), but proper names break the rule (*mid-Atlantic*, *un-American*).

Selfless is not hyphenated because in this case *self* is not a prefix; it's the main word with *-less* as the suffix.

Despite common usage, *vice-president* should be hyphenated; otherwise, it would seem to indicate the president of vice, just as *division president* (no hyphen) correctly indicates the president of the division.

Miscellaneous

- Do not hyphenate compounds with -ly adverbs like *wholly owned subsidiary*, *tightly knit organization*, *easily done lesson*, *especially nice house*, and many, many others. The -ly already does the job of relating the words. Confusion sometimes occurs because of -ly adjectives like *friendly* and *costly* that look like adverbs. These -ly words *do* take hyphens when used in a compound modifier: *friendly-looking man*, *costly-looking jewelry*.

- Remember that a hyphenated adjective compound used in front of the word it modifies (*a well-known man*, *a well-made desk*) is not hyphenated when it follows it (*the man is well known*, *the desk is well made*). Also: never write "the most well-known man"; simply say, "the best-known man." BUT: *well-being* is always hyphenated because it's a compound noun, not a compound adjective modifier.

- Use the hyphen to show combined duties: *secretary-treasurer*, *teacher-coach*, *owner-operator*.

- Use hyphens to indicate stuttering: *B-b-b-b-b-b-but wait!*

COLON

Page 84 The colon would also be used to introduce a vertical list in which the items are on separate lines. For both kinds of lists, however, a colon would not be used if the list items complete a sentence started by the introduction to the list:

> *In the old dusty box were*
>   *2,004 buttons*
>   *12,119 toothpicks*
>   *36,312 unmatched socks*
>   *1 diploma from the*
>   *Rothschild International*
>   *Washing Machine*
>   *Repair School*

Avoid the common error of using a semicolon for a colon:

WRONG: *He held three objects; a balloon, a wig, and a hat.*

RIGHT: *He held three objects: a balloon, a wig, and a hat.*

Miscellaneous

- The first word after a colon is not capitalized unless it is a name or if it starts a complete sentence.

- The colon (instead of a comma) is used to introduce a long quotation of two or more sentences.

- Use a colon after the character name in dramatic scripts:

  MILLICENT: No, I'm Millicent.
  FRED: Then I must be Fred!

- Use a colon to separate chapter from verse in Bible citations (*John 3:16*), hours from minutes (*3:45 P.M.*), and subtitles from titles (*Hanging Around: A Tale of Suspense*).

- The colon is placed outside the ending quotation mark or parenthesis.

- AGAIN: Avoid the common error of using a semicolon for a colon.

APOSTROPHE

Plurals of letters, numbers, and words as words

The apostrophe is used for plurals of
LETTERS Mind your *p*'s and *q*'s and dot your *i*'s.
NUMBERS Your *6*'s resemble *G*'s. During the 1960's (BUT: During the '60s [to avoid the extra apostrophe])
WORDS AS WORDS There are too many *onward*'s in your speech.

(N.B. In the examples above, although the letter or word may be italics, the *'s* is not.)

(Good authorities allow omission of the apostrophe in many such plurals [*1960s*, *three Rs*], but to ensure consistency and easy decision-making, it's best to follow the traditional style as described.)

All other plurals need no apostrophes unless they have internal periods:

The Smiths have two Marys in the family.

He earned two Ph.D.'s and six IOUs.

Miscellaneous

- The possessives of organization names often omit the apostrophe:

  Western Pilots Association

  Aggawam State Teachers College

- For compound possessives, it's *sister-in-law's house* and *sisters-in-law's houses*.

- Use the apostrophe to show omission of letters when reproducing pronunciation:

  We're a-goin' now, y'all. G'bye!

PARENTHESES AND BRACKETS

Placement of punctuation

- Punctuation with parentheses and brackets is placed in relation to the sentence meaning:

  In the sentence you are now reading (in which this parenthetical remark is included), the comma goes outside the ending parenthesis (and so does the ending period).

  (However, a separate sentence completely inside parentheses like this one keeps the ending period inside.)

- The same logic applies to other punctuation:

  There was never a question (or was there?) of money.

  Did he say there was never *(I bet he said "seldom"!) a question of money?*

Miscellaneous

- The first word of a sentence in parentheses within another sentence is not capitalized—even if it's a complete sentence (unless the first word is a proper noun).

- When numbering or lettering a series within a paragraph, don't use the single parenthesis mark: *1)*; it's not quickly read. Use both the beginning and ending marks:

  He suggested (1) that he be given carte blanche, or (2) that he be given free rein; but he couldn't decide which.

- Parentheses are used to confirm a spelled-out number:

  The price is eight dollars ($8).

- If you wish to include a comment that supposedly reflects a character's thought, enclose it in parentheses:

  They entered Antoine's Restaurant leading four elephants ("Aren't we interesting!") and asked for a table near some hay.

- Use parentheses to enclose a helpful translation of a foreign word or phrase:

  Horrified, Bill remembered that the word nugatory *comes from the Latin* nugae *(trifles).*

DASH

Page 120 Although the dash is used to set off words in ways similar to the use of commas and parentheses, there is a difference.

The **dash** warns the reader of a strong interruption in thought. It calls strong attention to the set-off matter.

The **comma** sets off matter in a routine, closely connected way.

Parentheses only incidentally add information; they are the weakest of the three.

Compare:

There was only one thing—money—that was needed.

There was only one thing, money, that was needed.

There was only one thing (money) that was needed.

Miscellaneous

• Use the dash in dialogue to indicate an unfinished sentence:

Suddenly, Sam cried, "Look out, Bill! He's going to shoo—" [no period]

"If I thought for one minute—," he began. [comma is used]

• Use the dash in front of the source after an epigraph:

I came, I saw, I left.
    —Julius Fenwick

- Dashes can be used in place of numbers or letters to introduce items in a list:

  The logic was this:—Things fall off the kitchen table.—They fall down.—Gravity must be in the linoleum.

Note that the first word in each item is capitalized and that each item ends with a period.

QUOTATION MARKS

Very long quotations

If a long paragraph or more is being quoted, do not use quotation marks. Instead, skip a line and indent both sides of the quoted material. When the quotation is completed, skip a line and resume the full margins.

Quotation marks vs. italics

Italicize names of

periodicals	record albums
books	paintings, statues
story collections	ships, trains, planes, spacecraft
plays	
long compositions	
long poems	
TV series names	
movies	

Quote names of
articles, essays
book chapters and parts
short stories
songs
short poems
TV series segments

Certain famous books and documents are neither italicized nor quoted. Examples are: the Bible and its books, the Koran, the Magna Carta, the Constitution of the United States, the Bill of Rights, the Declaration of Independence, and others.

If it is not awkward to include *The* or *A* or *An* before a title, do so; otherwise, it is not necessary, even if it's part of the title.

Miscellaneous

American usage puts the comma and period *inside* the quotation marks, double or single. British usage does not—which was probably one of King George's ideas.

Selected References

The Associated Press Style Book and Libel Manual. Rev. ed. Edited by Christopher W. French. Reading, MA: Addison-Wesley Publishing Co., Inc., 1987.

The Chicago Manual of Style. 13th ed. Chicago: University of Chicago Press, 1982.

Prentice Hall Handbook for Writers. 10th ed. Edited by Richard S. Beal and others. Englewood Cliffs, NJ: Prentice Hall, 1988.

Webster's Guide to Abbreviations. Springfield, MA: Merriam-Webster Inc., 1985.

Good sources that are commonly available are the punctuation guides in such dictionaries as:

American Heritage Dictionary: Second College Edition. Boston: Houghton Mifflin Company, 1982.

Webster's Third New International Dictionary of the English Language, Unabridged. Springfield, MA: Merriam-Webster Inc., 1981.

Index

About the Author/Illustrator

Stan Malotte is a former magazine and newspaper editor, educational film writer/producer, and teacher. He lives in California.